DOT TO DOT FOR KIDS AGES 4-8

SPLENDID YOUTH

THIS BOOK BELONGS TO:

_____

SNAIL

2 DOLPHIN 2

3 GRASSHOPPER

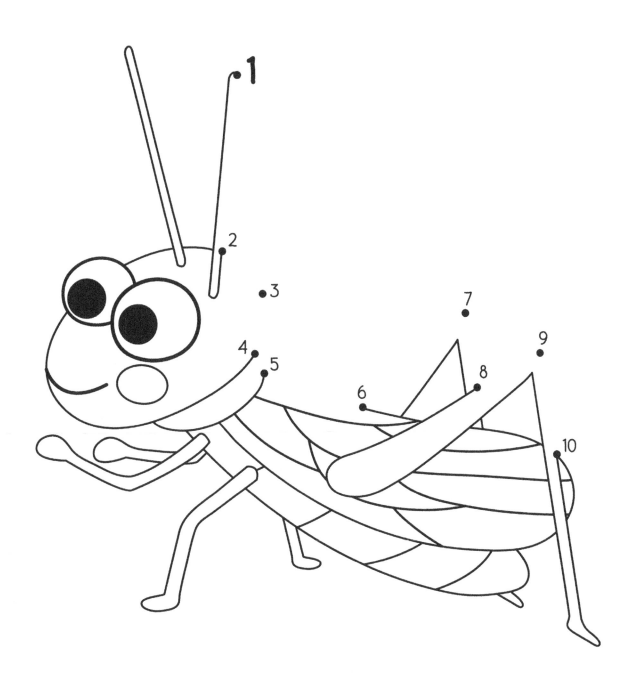

4 GOLF CART 4

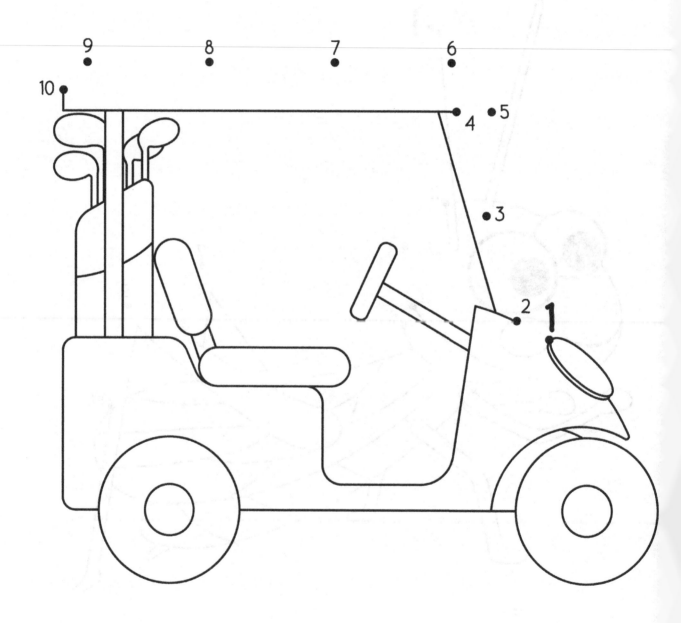

LAPTOP

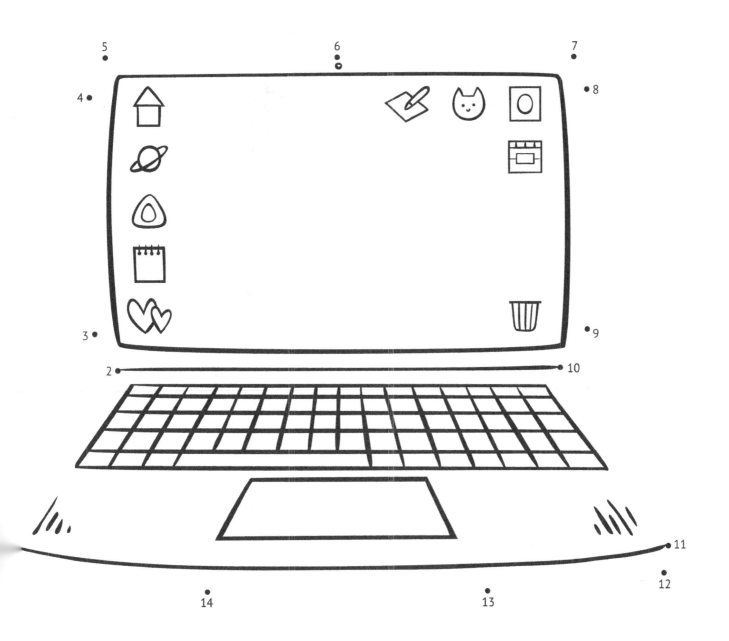

FROG

CHICK

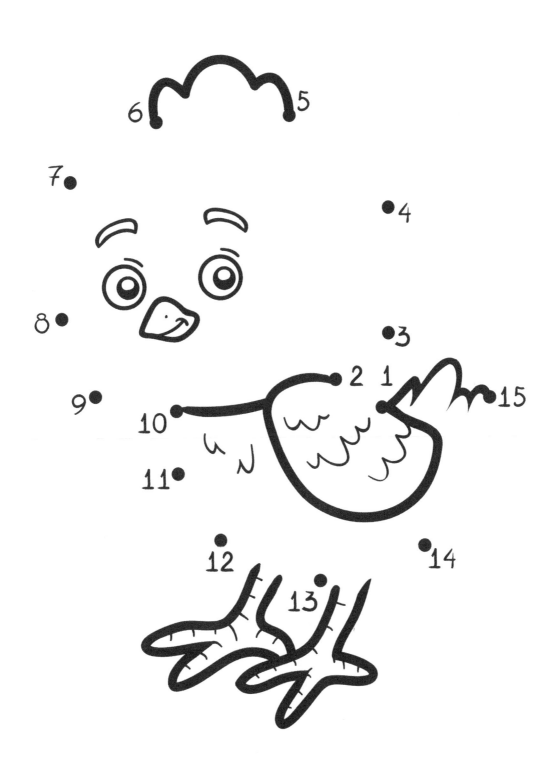

CANOE

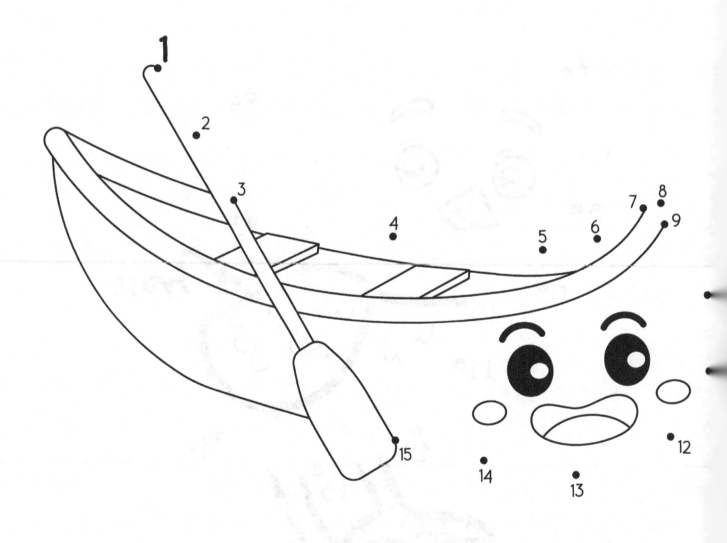

ROCKET

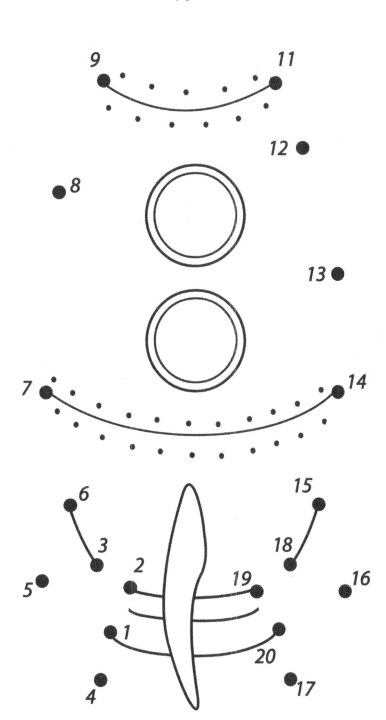

SHIRT

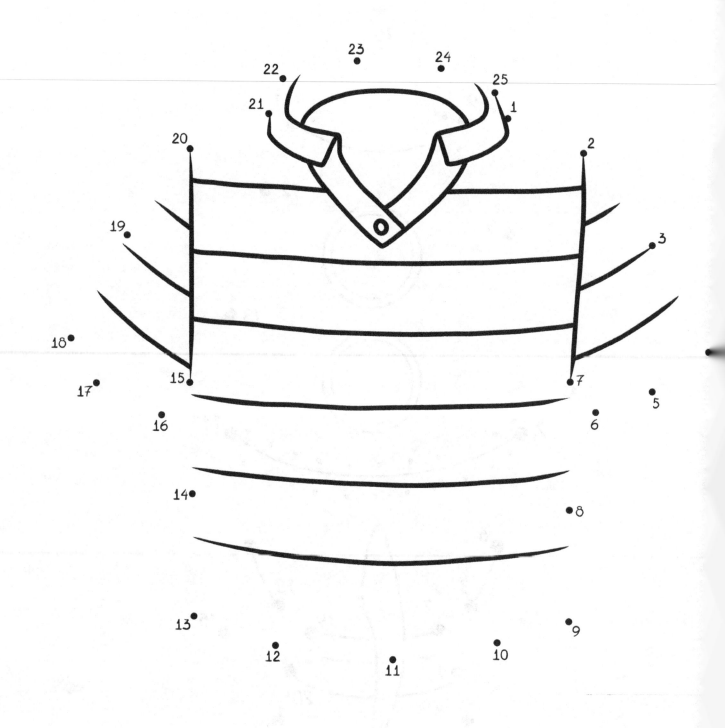

KIWI

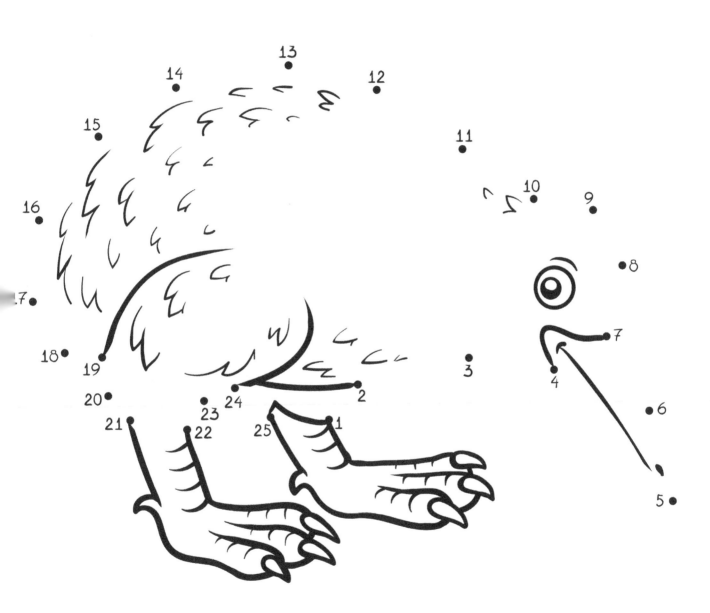

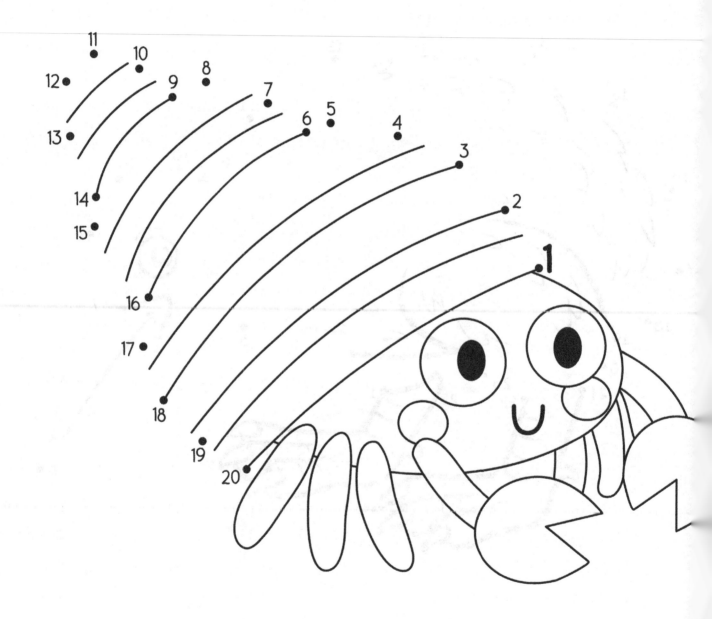

13 WATERMELON 13

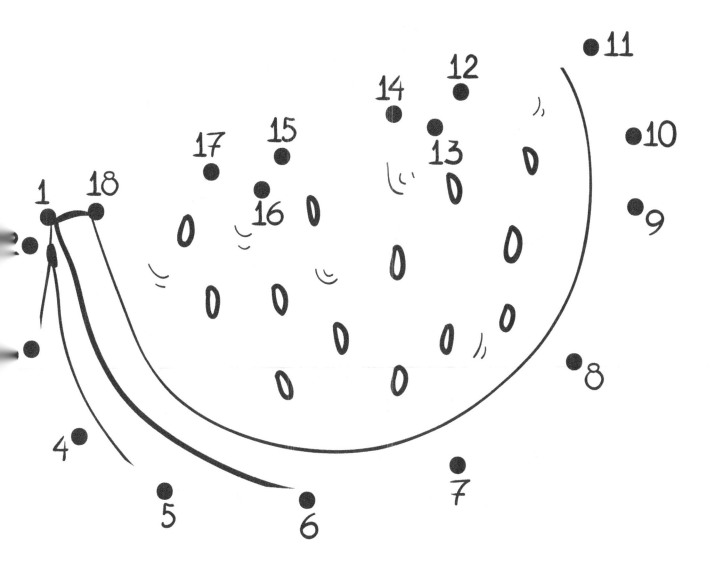

MUFFIN

BICYCLE

PRAM

FORKLIFT

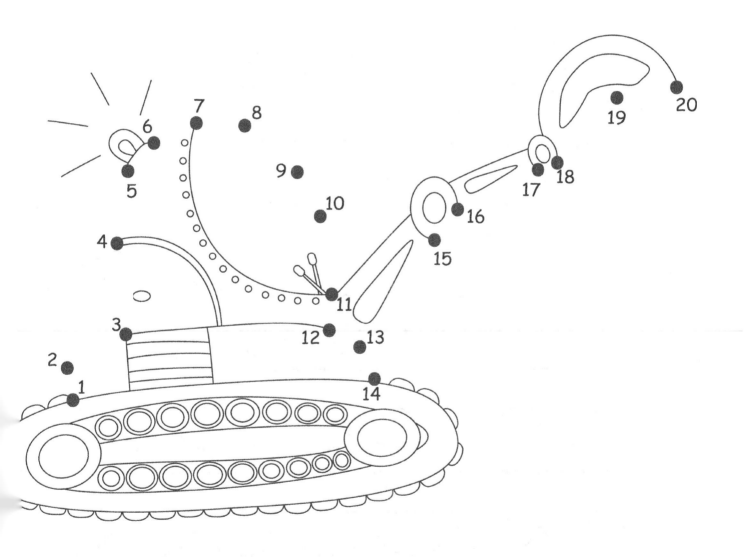

SHIP

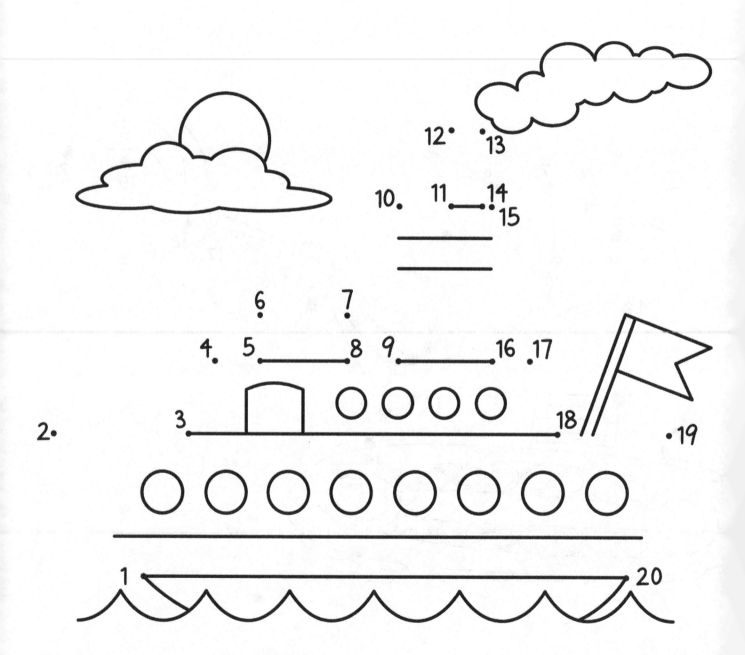

BOOT

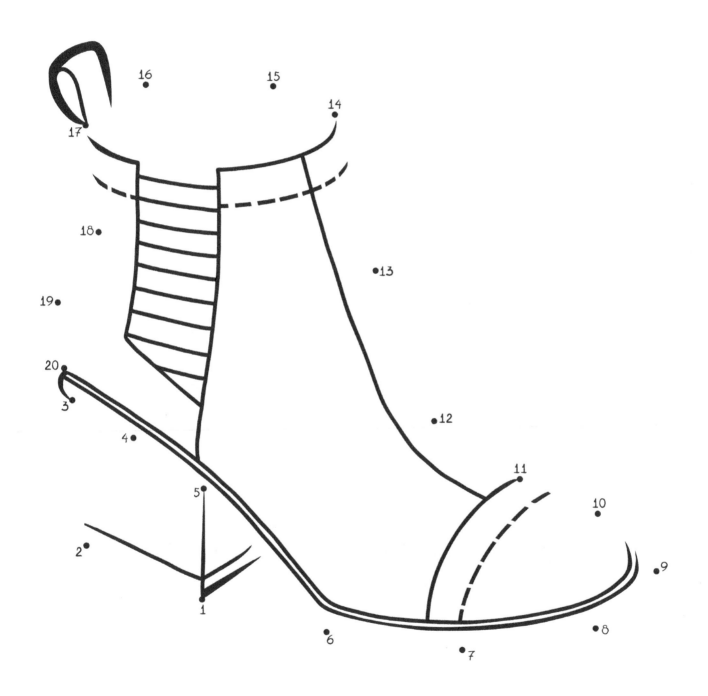

ANT

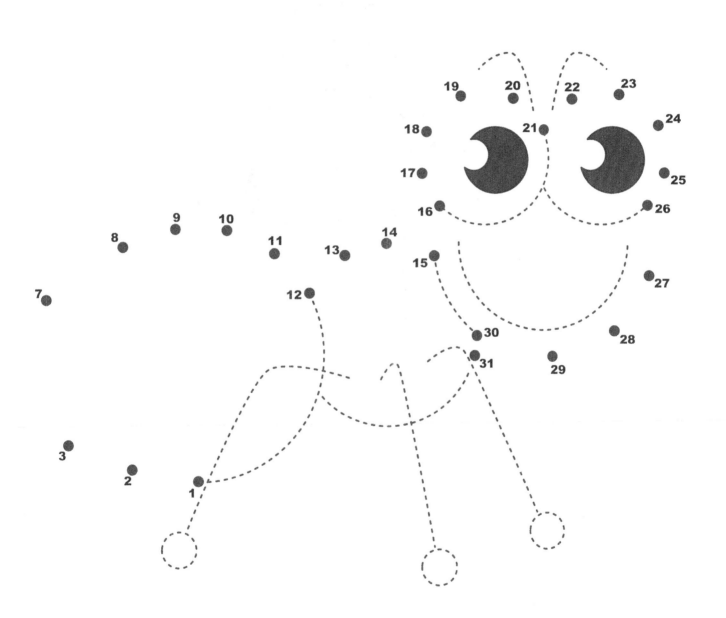

LAMP

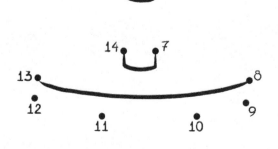

HELICOPTER

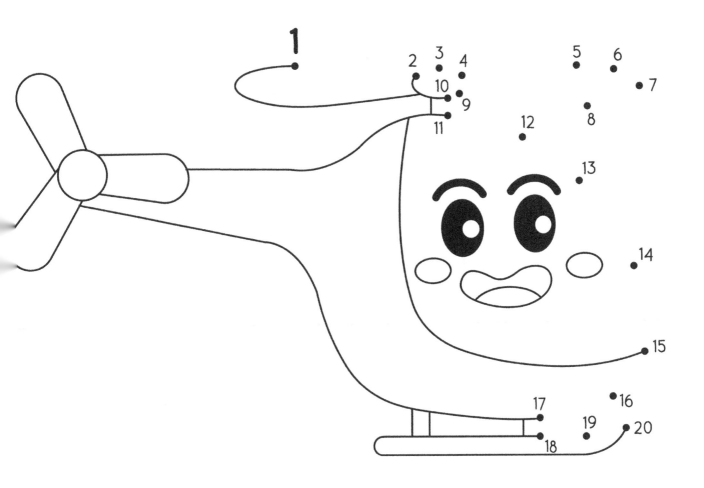

FLAMINGO

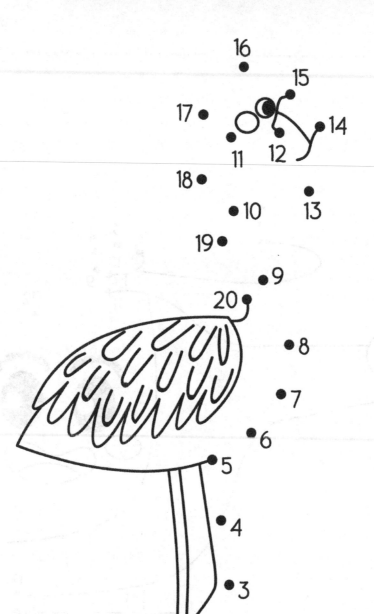

BOBSLEIGH

HANDCAR

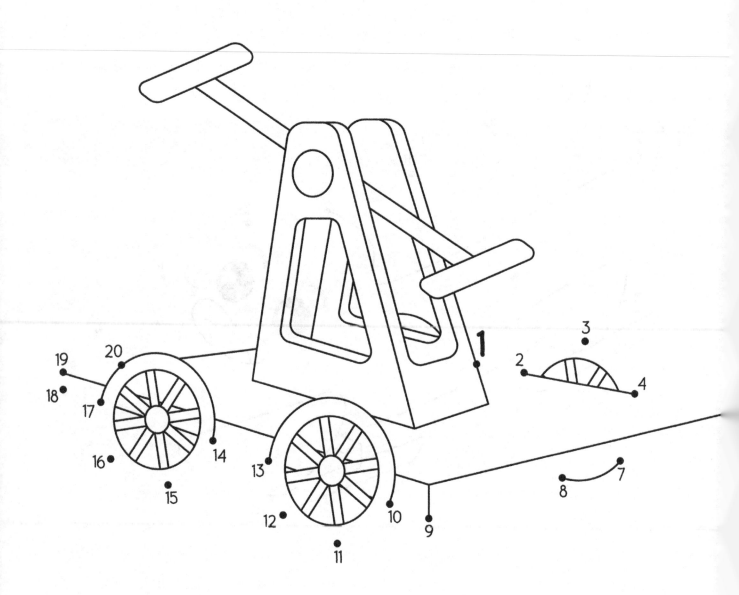

LORRY

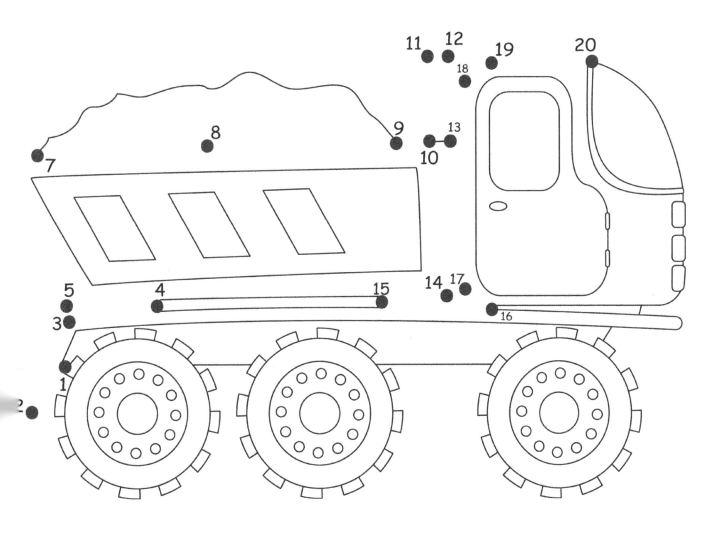

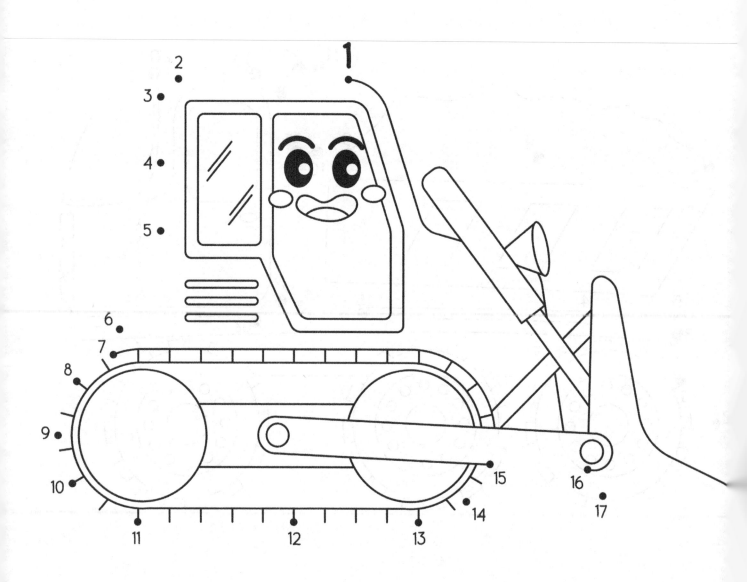

CAR

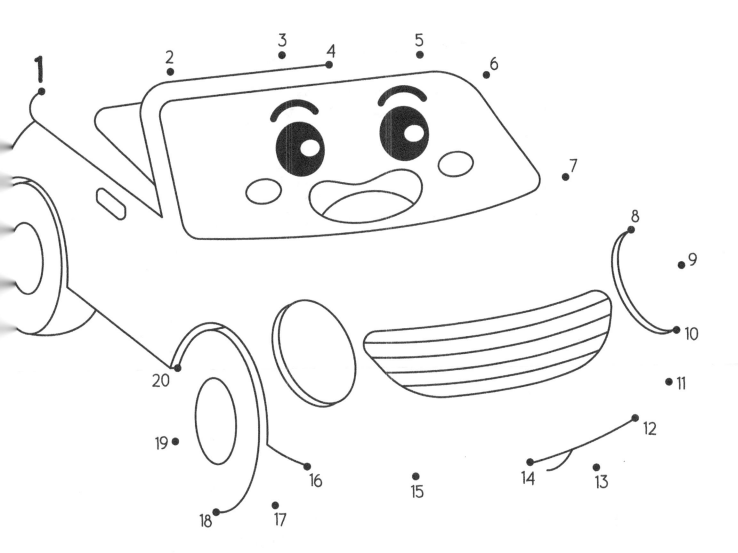

TOASTER

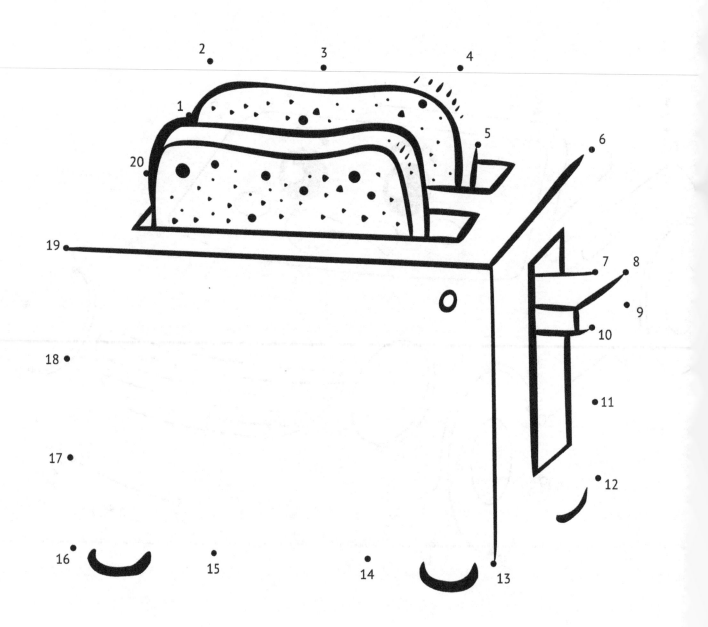

PENGUIN

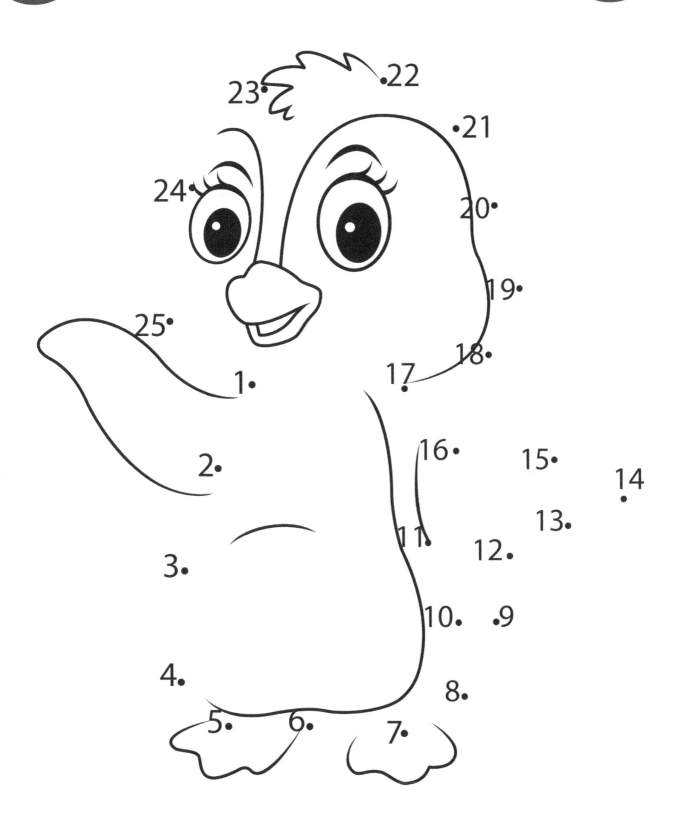

SKI LIFT

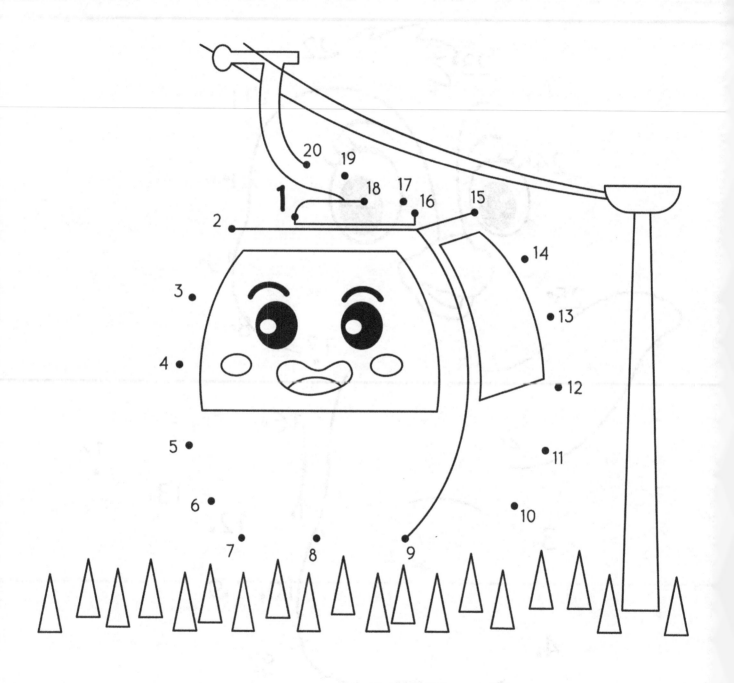

AMBULANCE

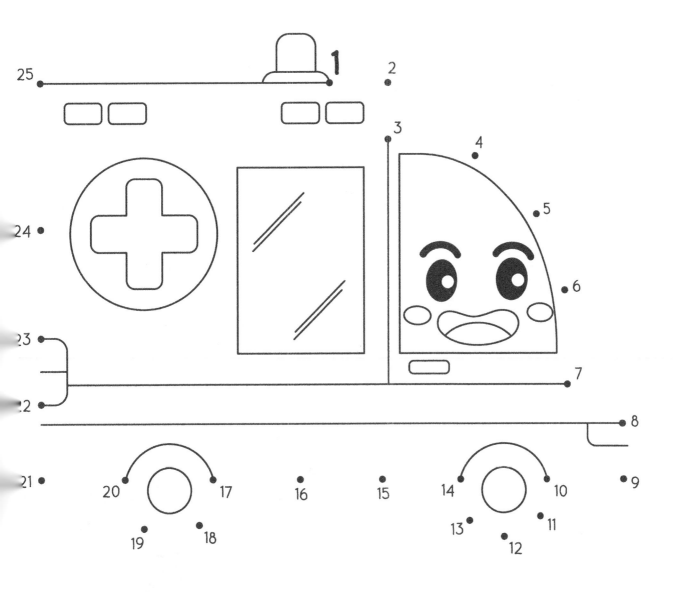

GO-CART

34

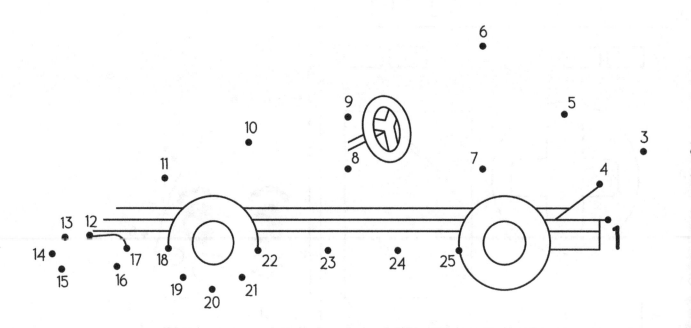

6

9
10
5
3
11
8
7
4
13 12
14
17 18 22
23 24 25
1
15 16
19 21
20

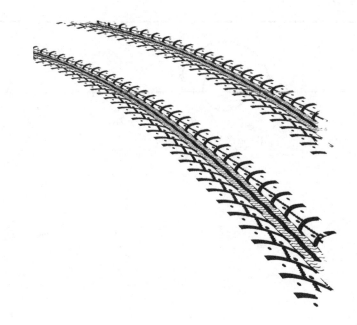

SUN

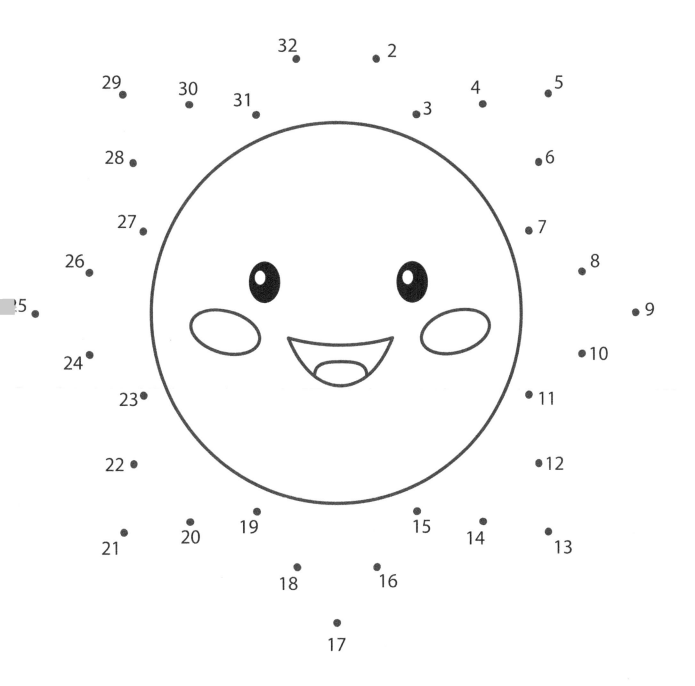

TURKEY

DOG

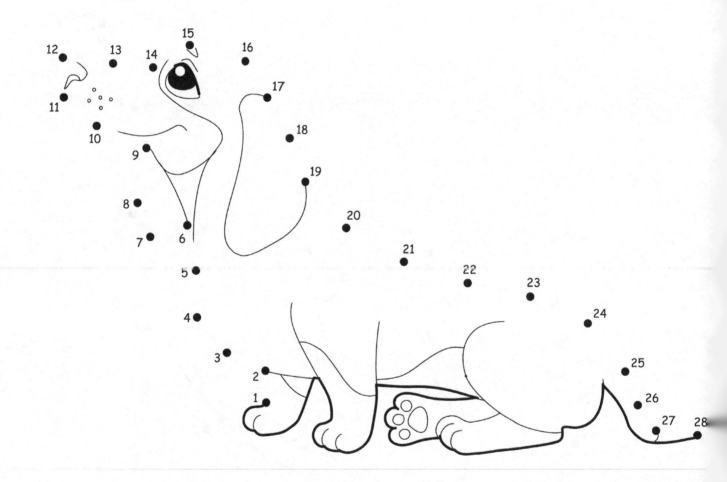

DODO

JELLYFISH

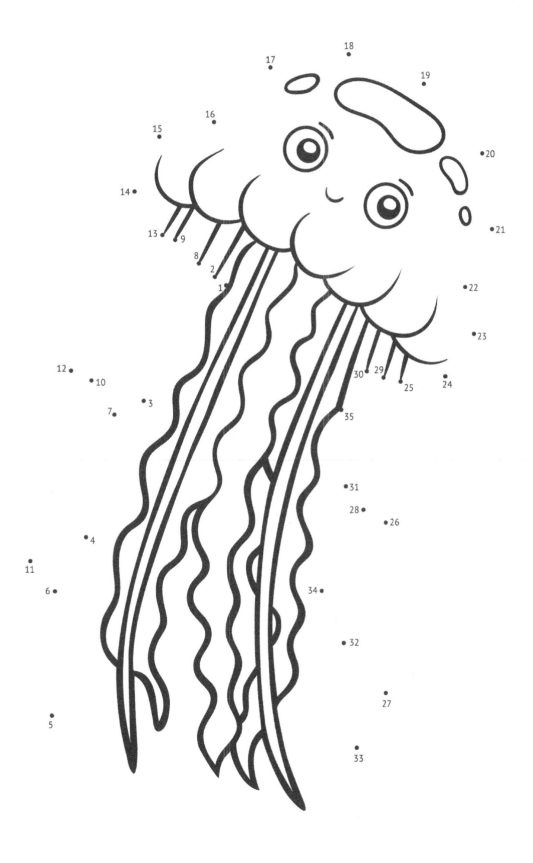

MOTORBIKE

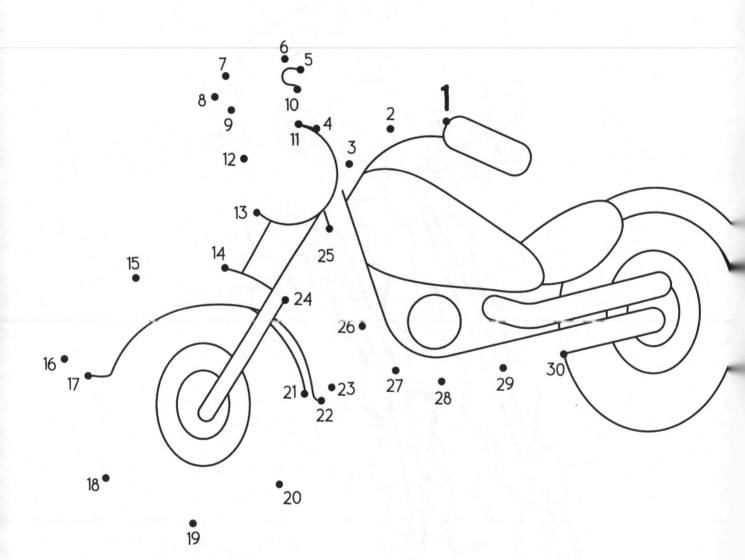

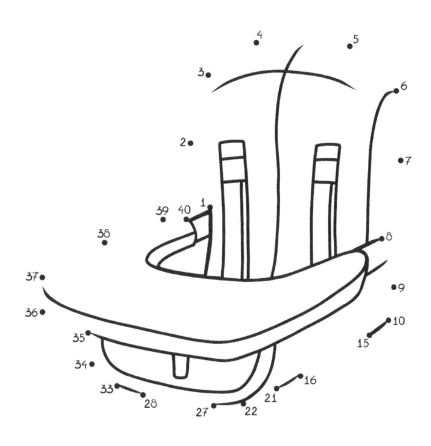

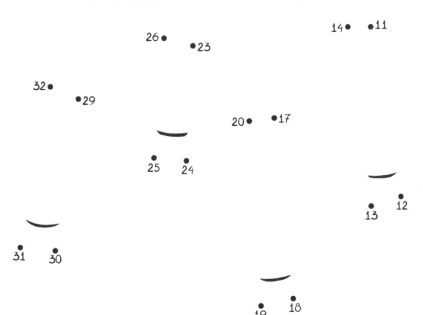

COOKER

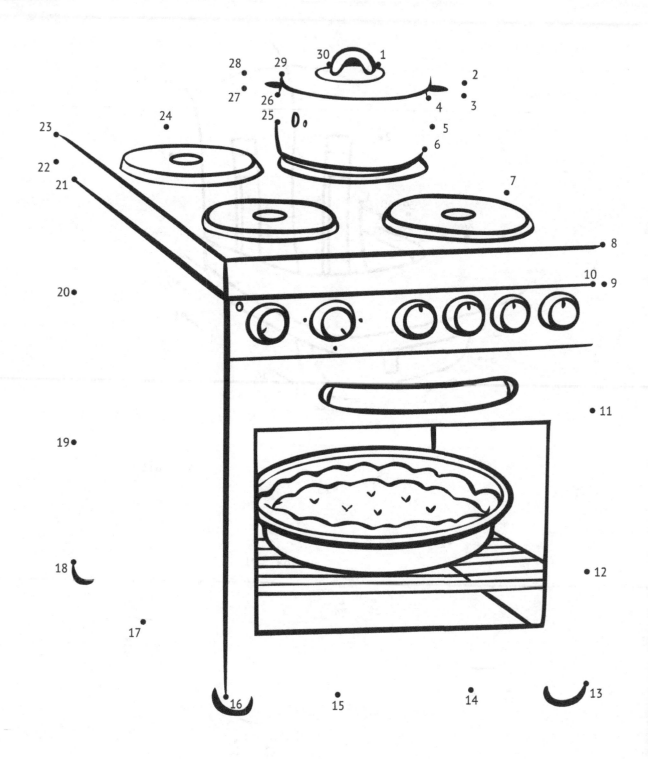

28
29
30
1
27
26
2
3
24
25
4
23
5
22
6
21
7
8
10
9
20
11
19
18
12
17
16
15
14
13

BELLS

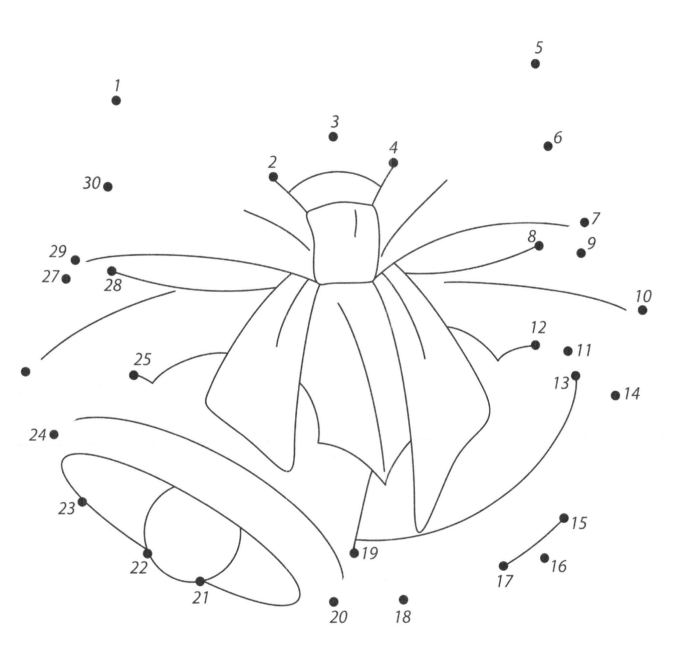

PLANE

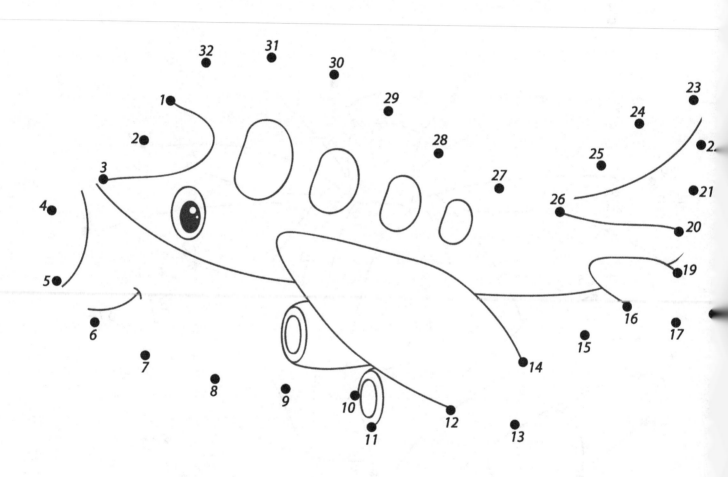

TOUCAN

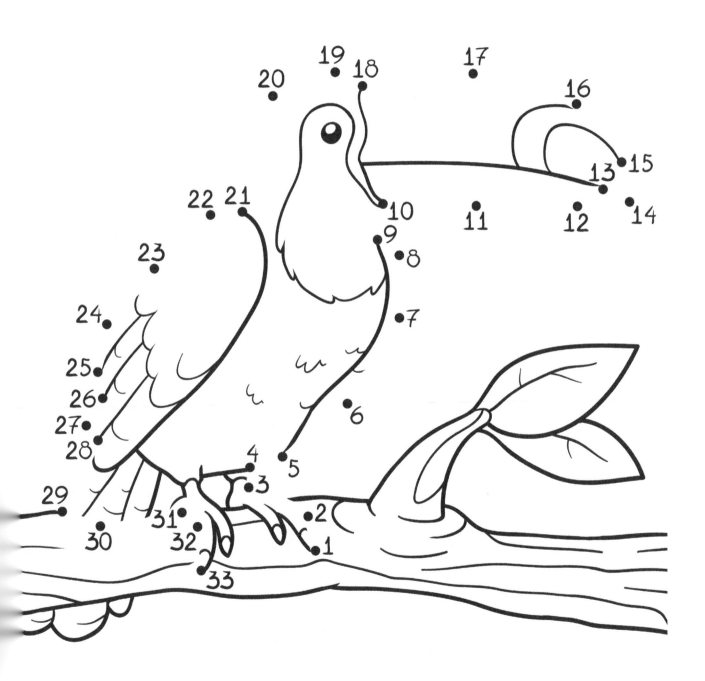

POODLE

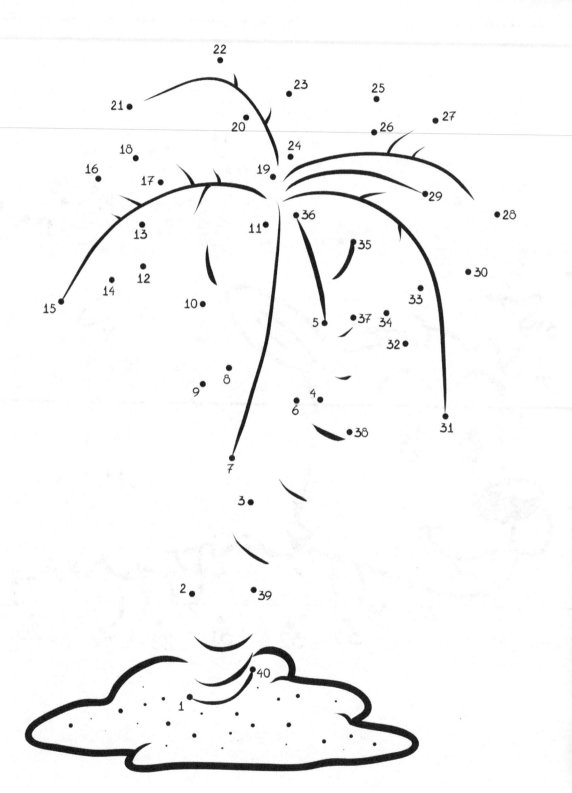

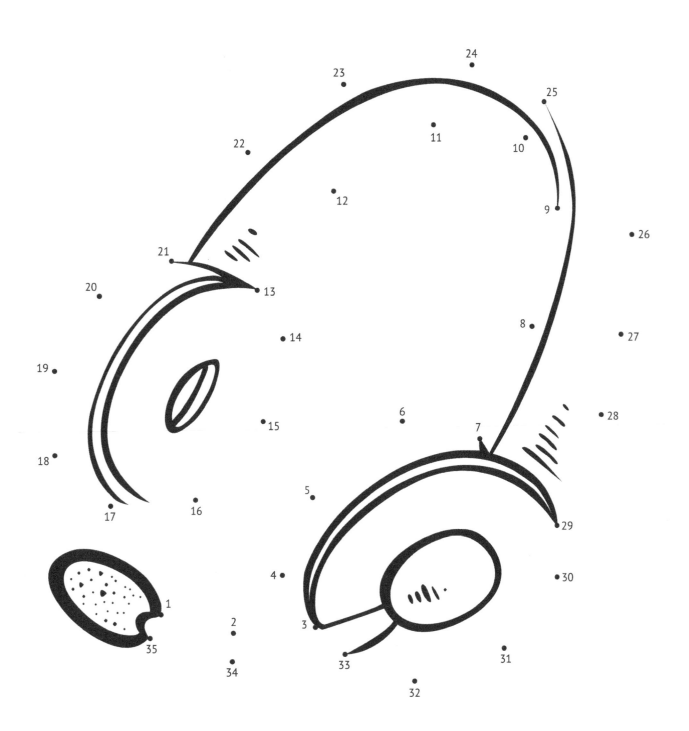

APPLE

STRAWBERRY

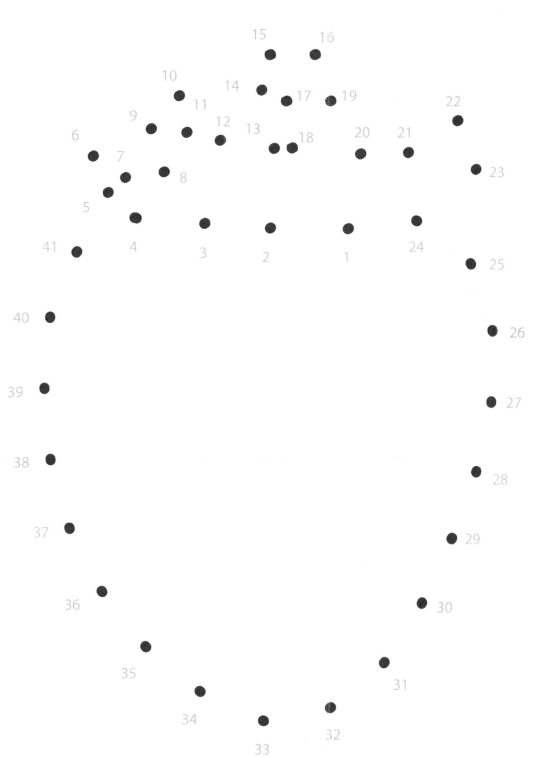

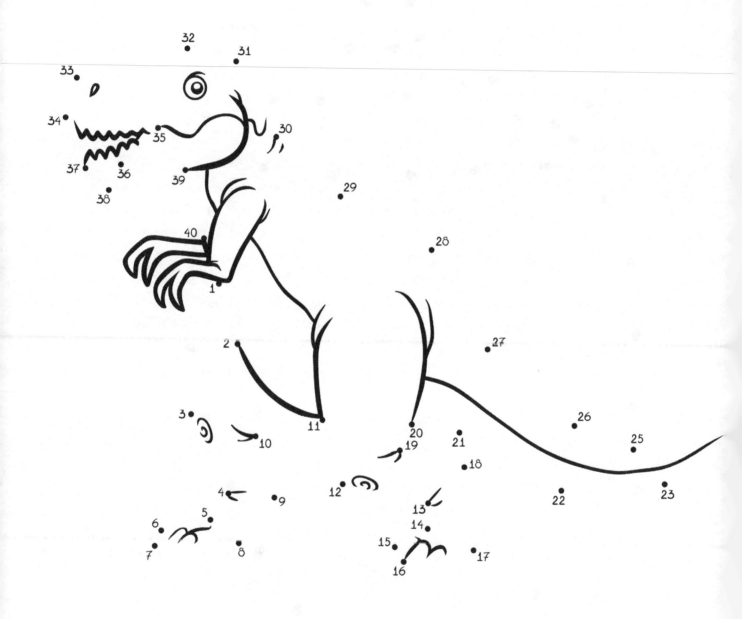

PEACOCK

 # CINGULATA

X-MAS TREE

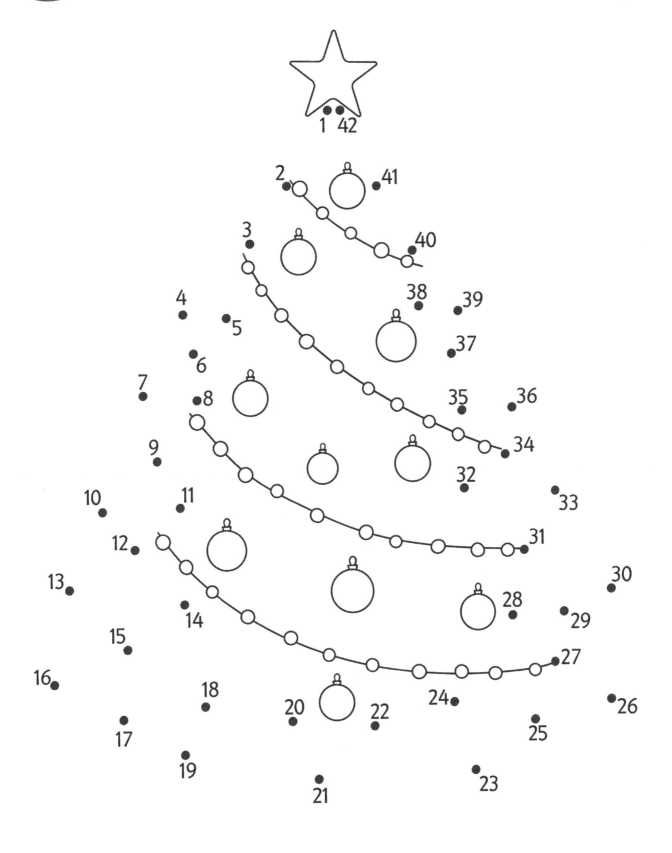

BANANA

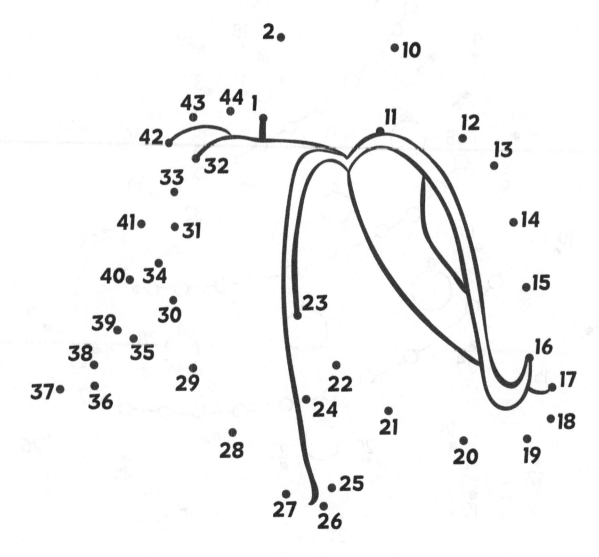

STARFISH

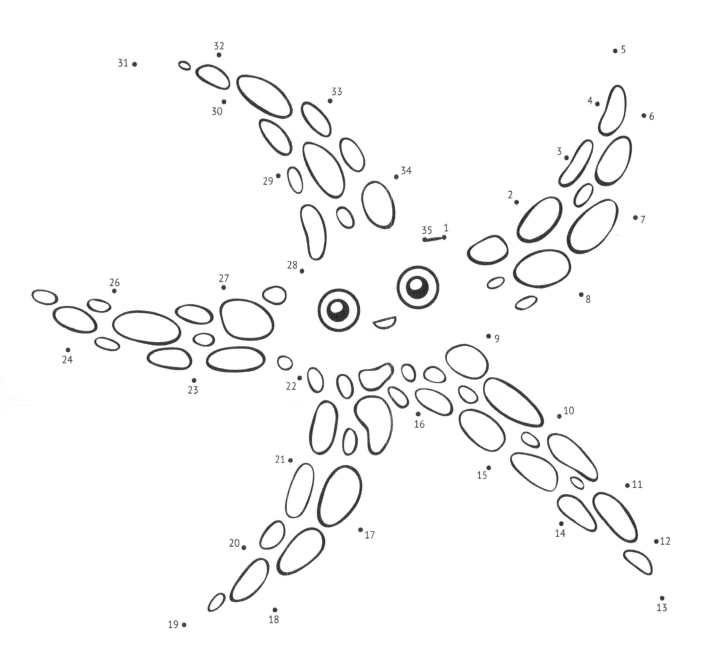

FISH

TELESCOPE

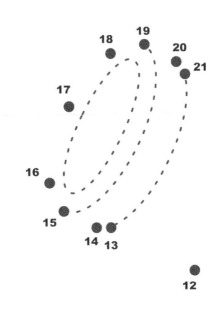
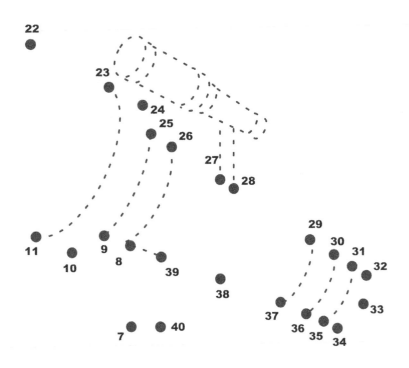
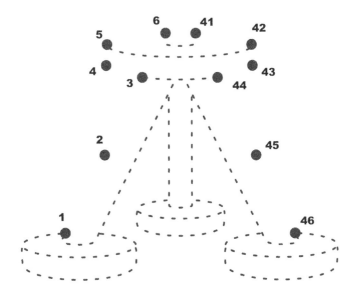

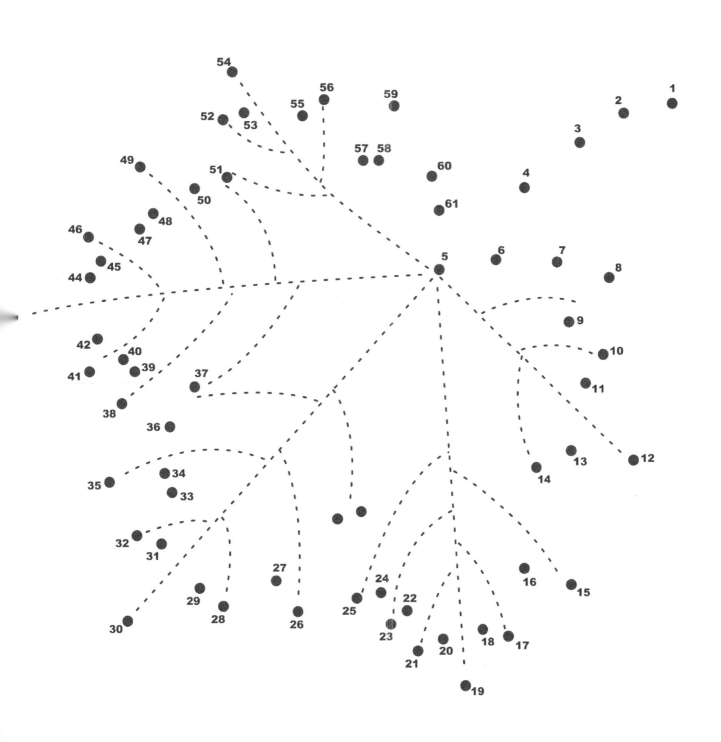

PIG

CRAB

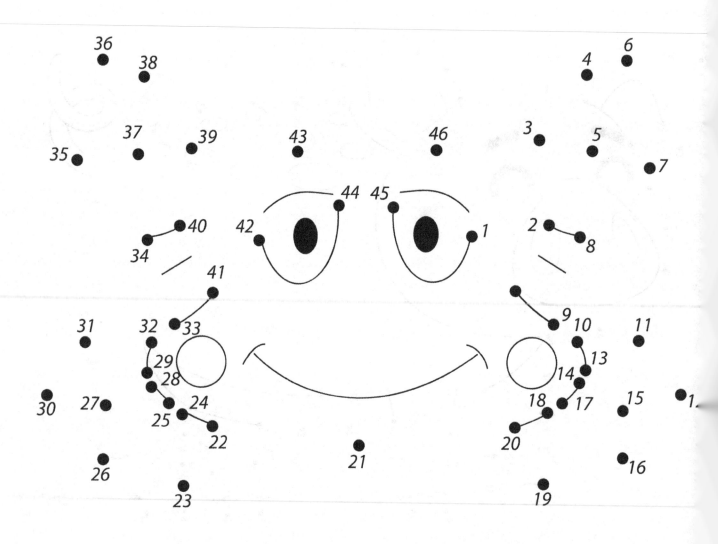

BEAR

TURTLE

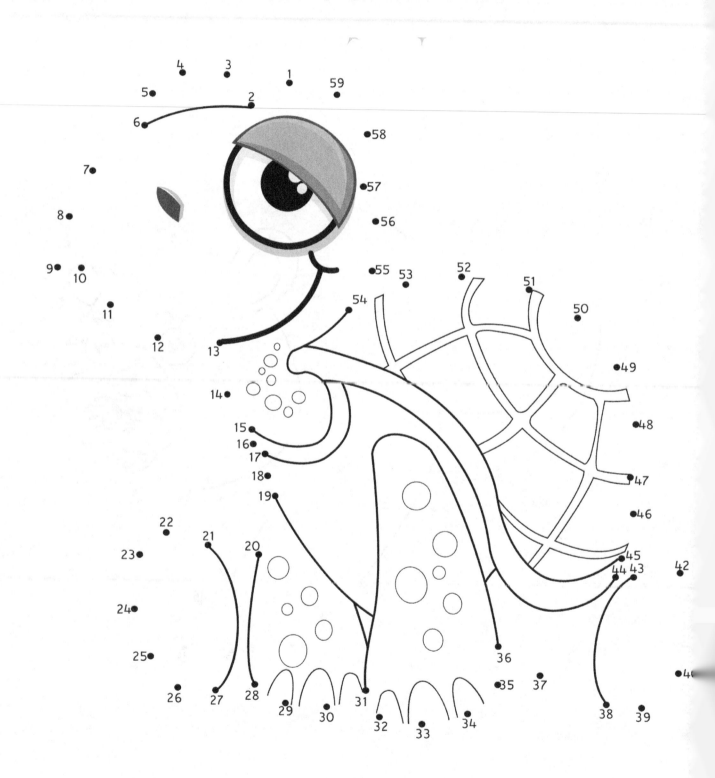

WHALE

TIGER

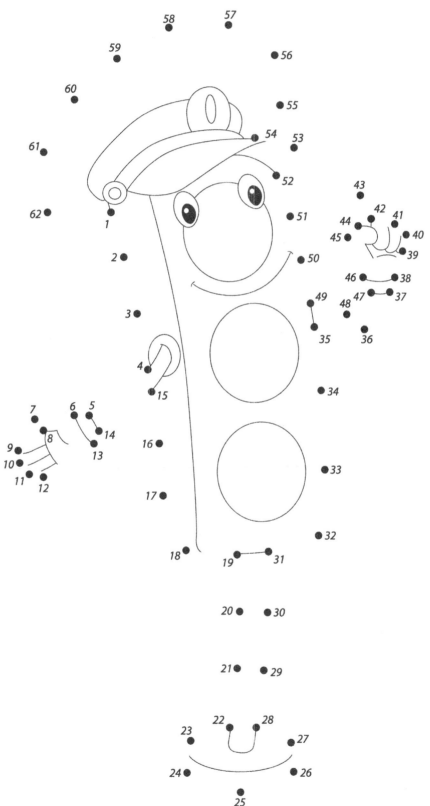

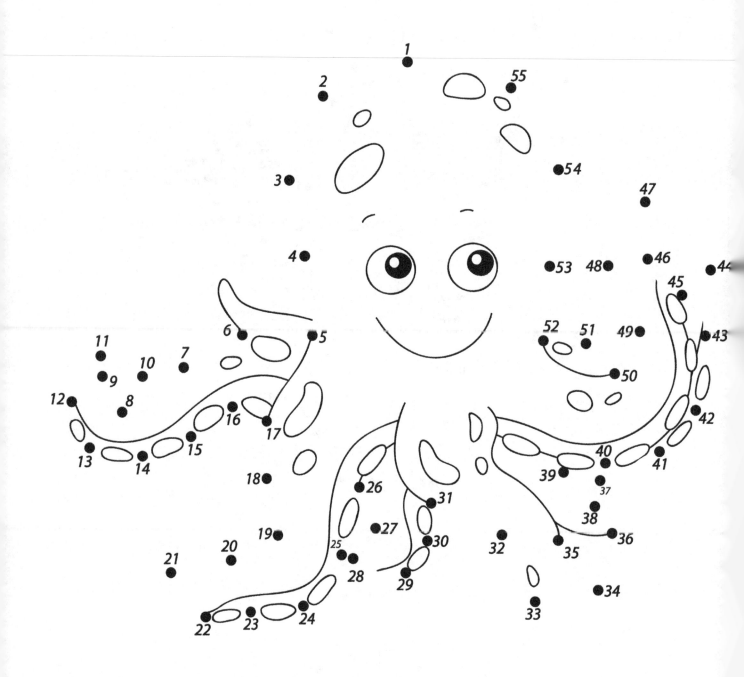

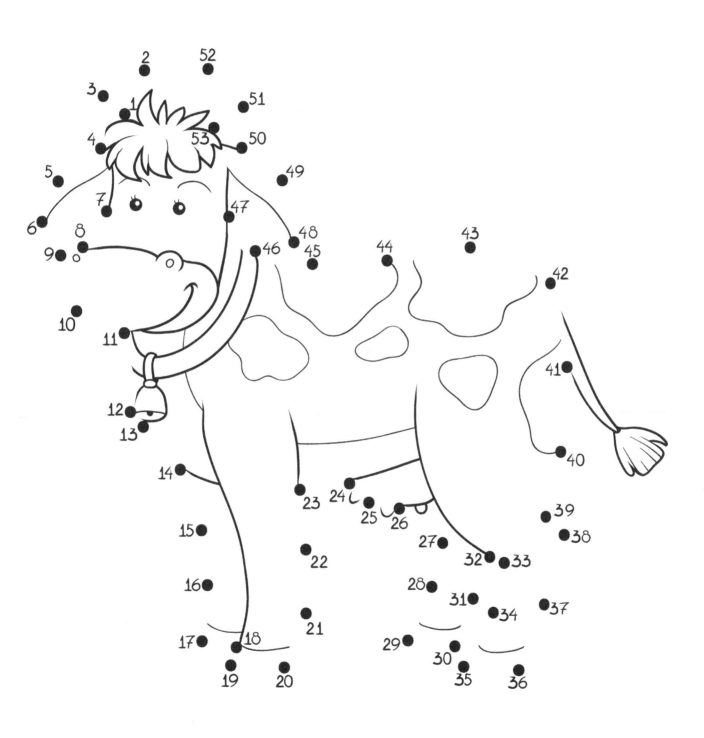

EAGLE

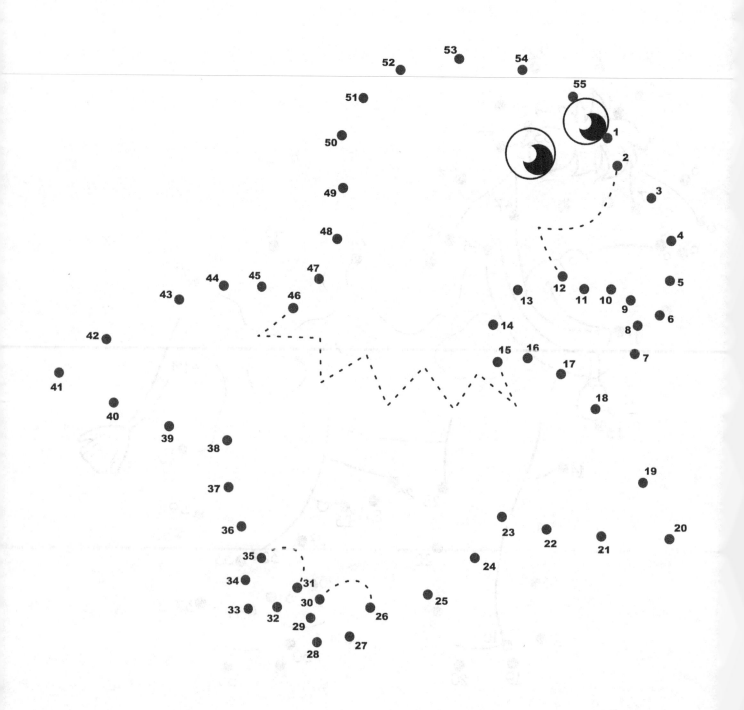

GOLDFISH

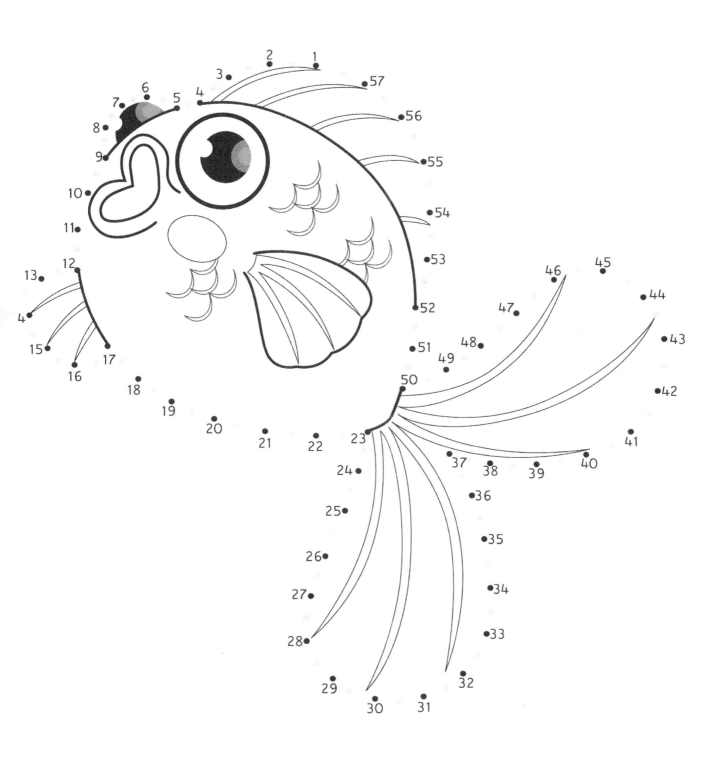

RAT

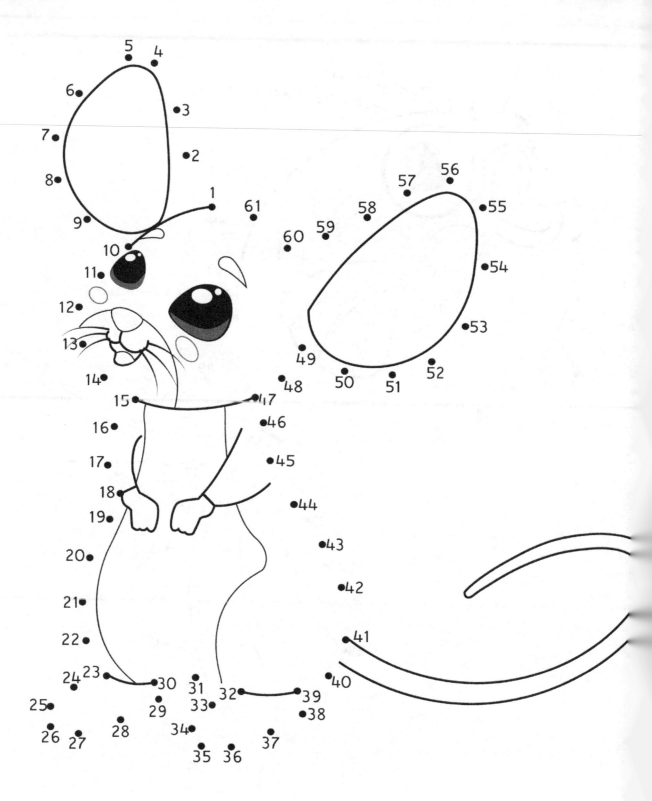

GIRAFFE

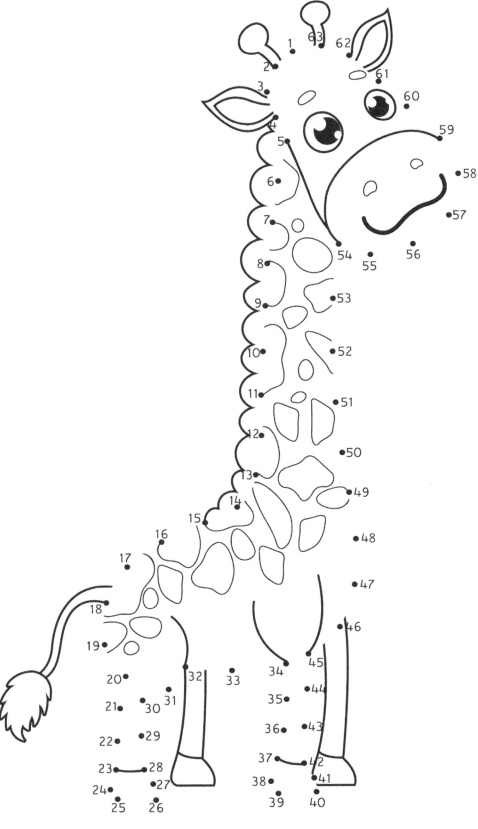

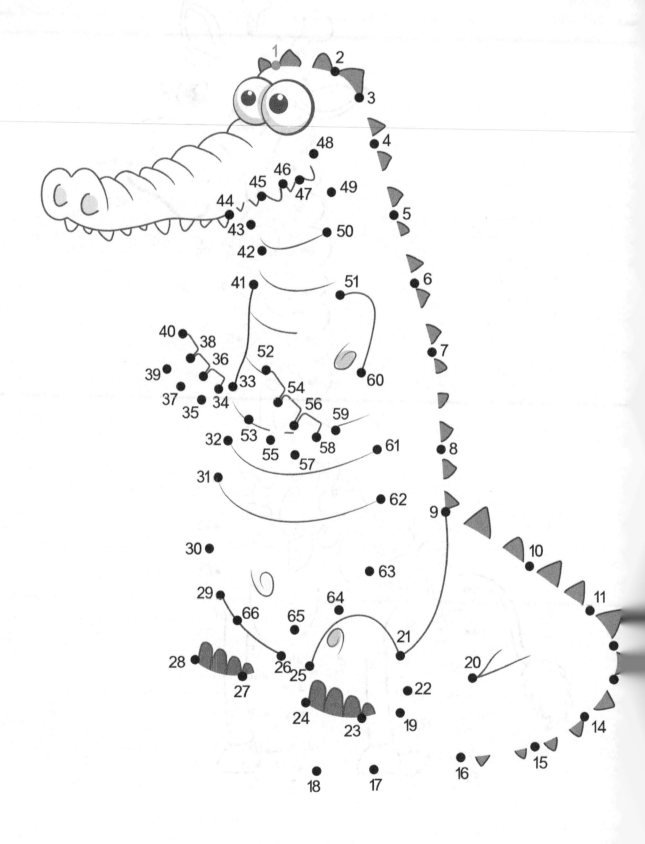

SHARK

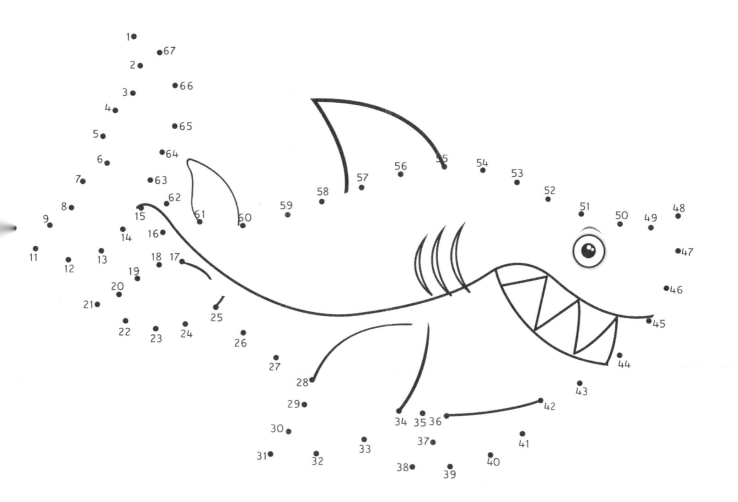

RABBIT

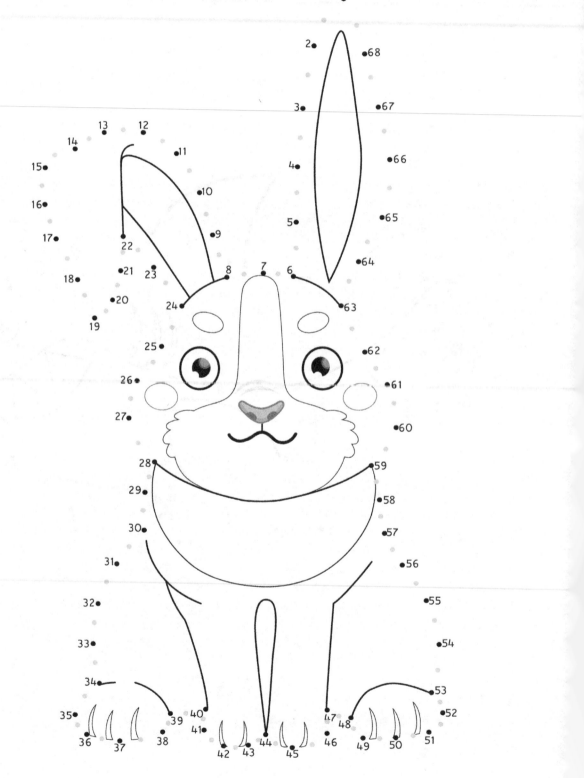

HIPPO

KOALA

BUTTERFLY

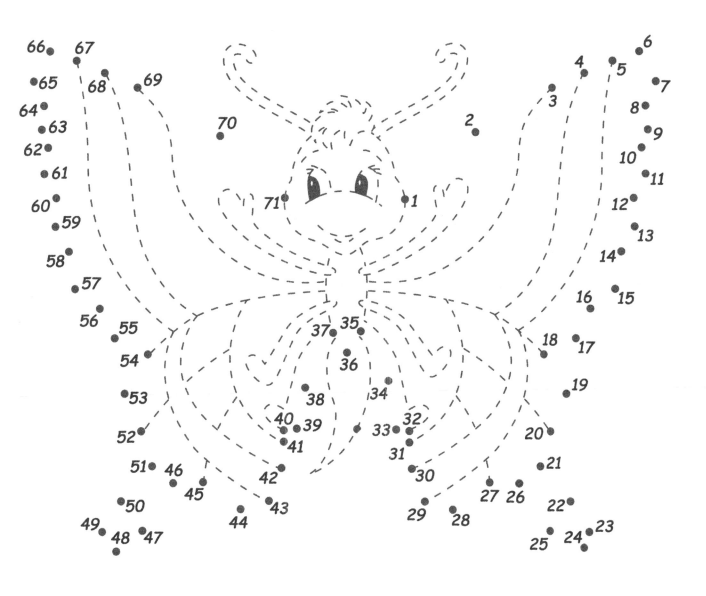

BATS

CAT

PUPPY

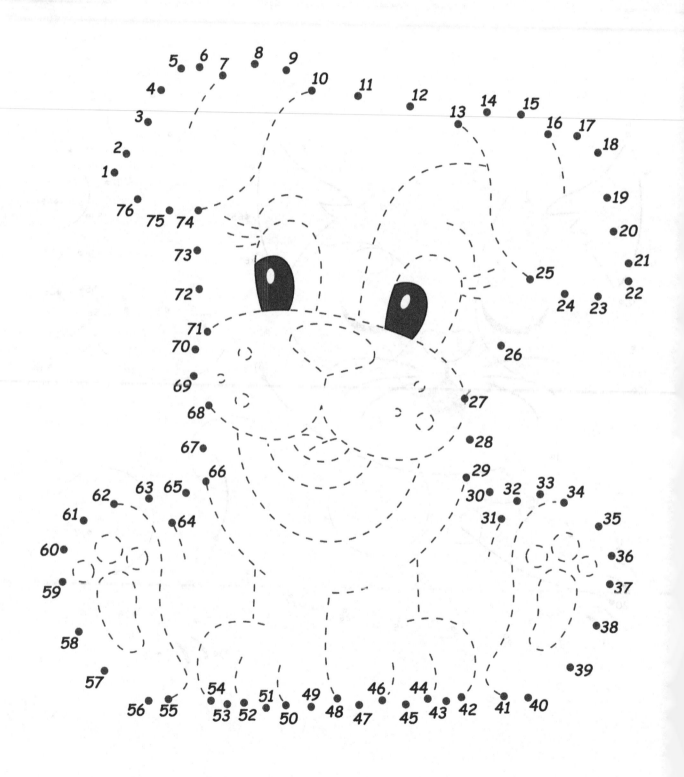

SQUIRREL

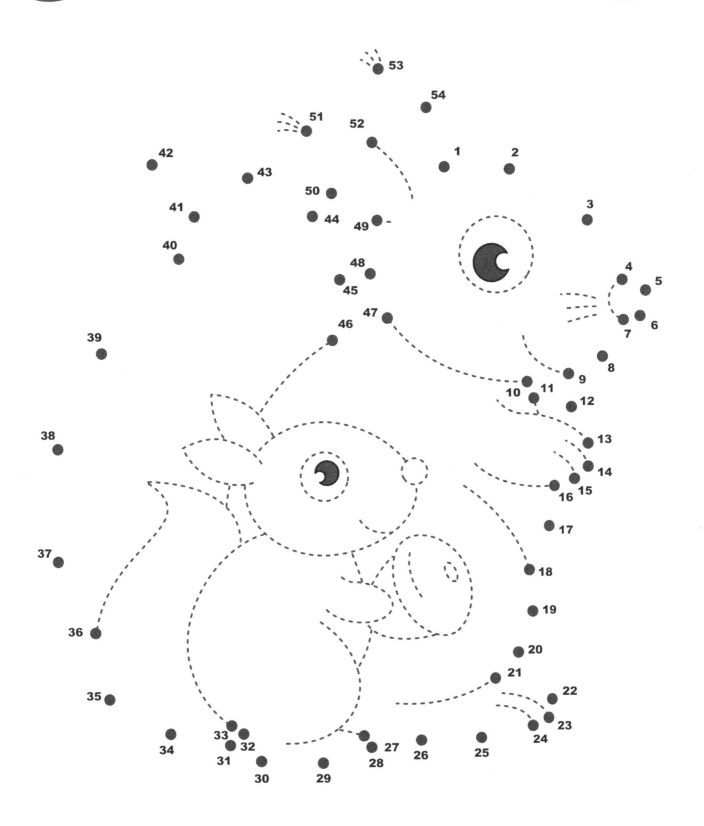

CHICKEN

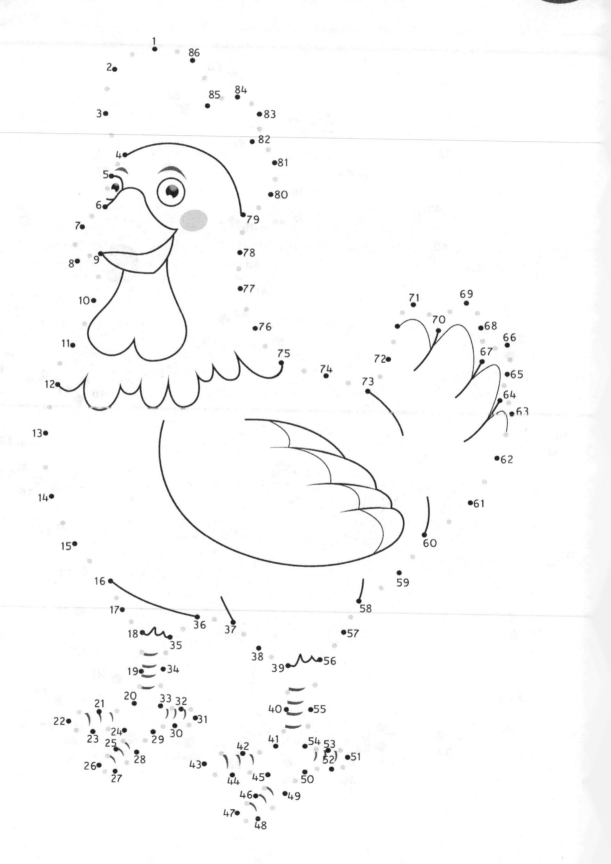

PANDA

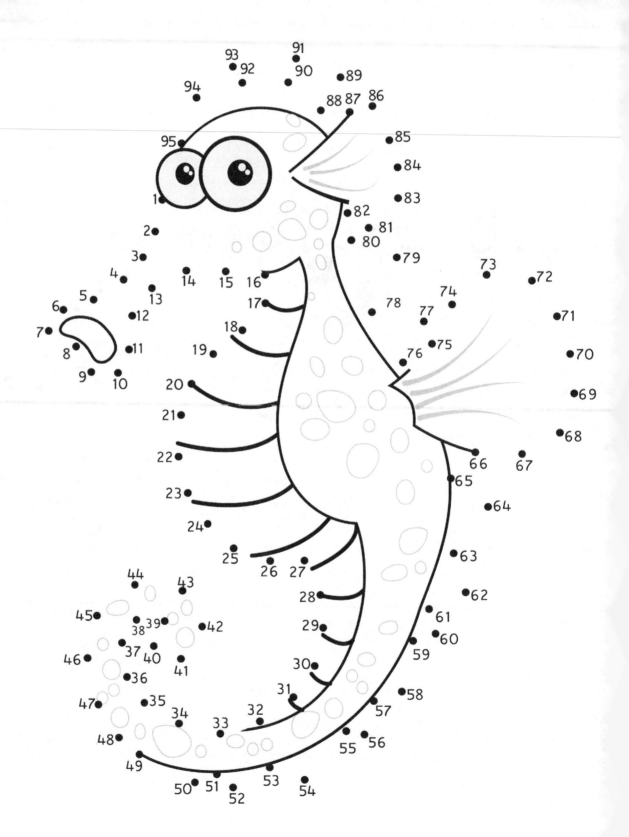

OSTRICH

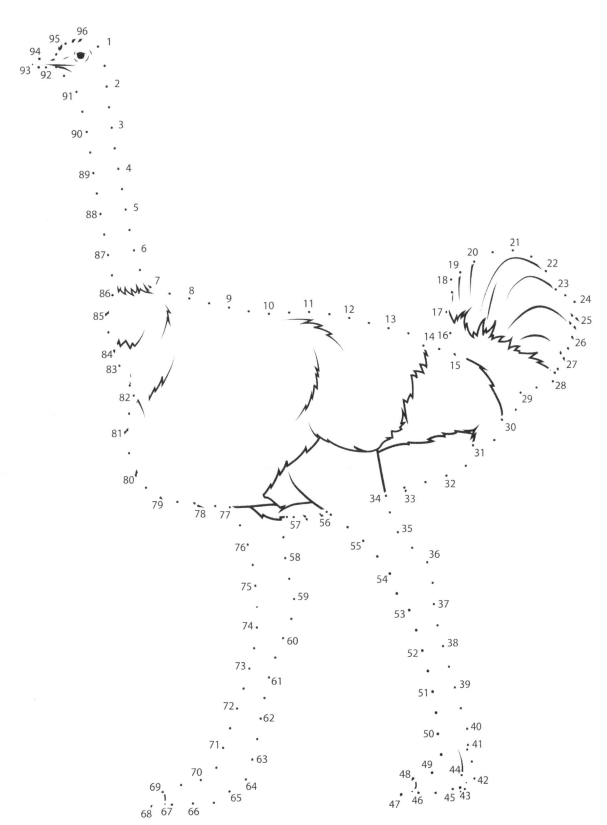

SNOWMAN

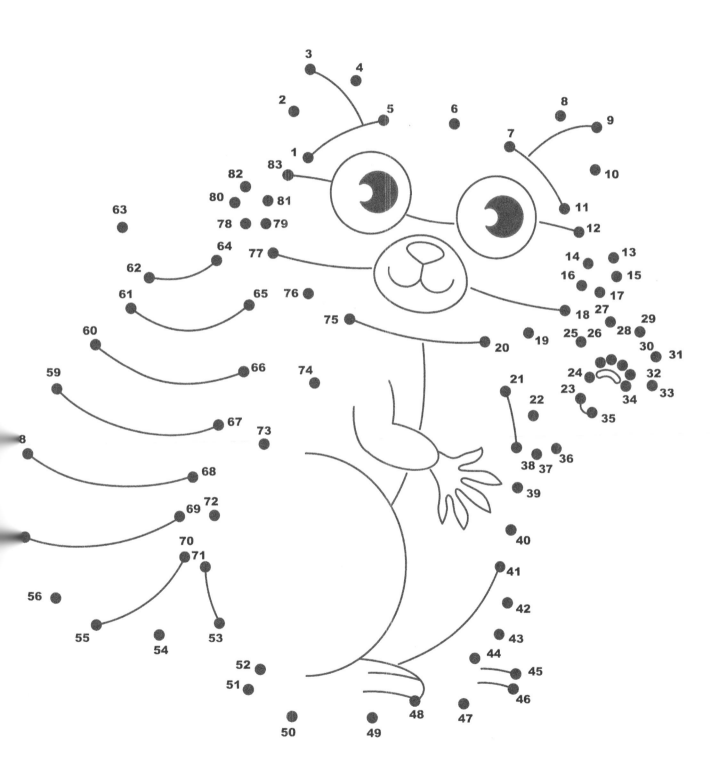

MERMAID

ELK

99

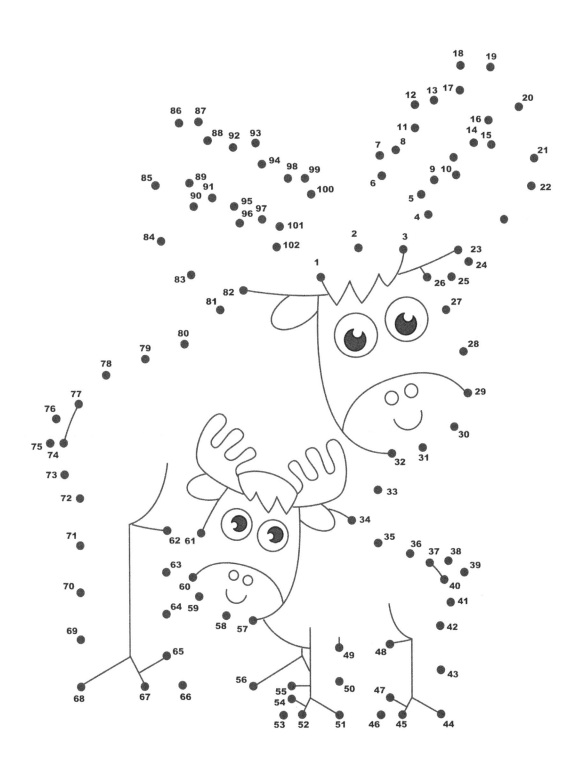

SNAKE

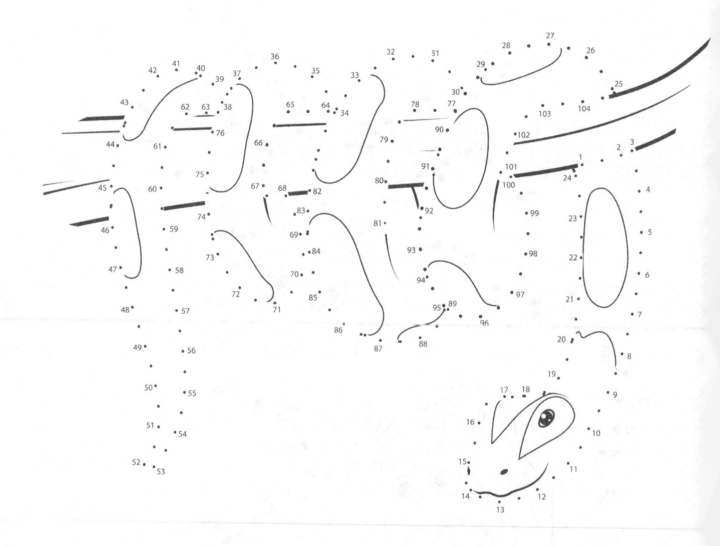

CONGRATULATIONS

HAS COMPLETED THIS BOOK!

Made in the USA
Monee, IL
06 January 2025

76054717R00057